THE

CONFLICT:

Supposed to be

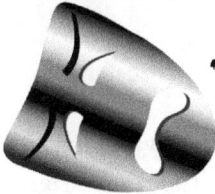

- VS -

The Wanna be

Keith Tucker

Dedication

This book is dedicated to the memory of one of the greatest women to ever walk this earth. She was a prime example of sacrifice, love, patience, forgiveness, kindness and generosity. She always looked for the good in people and rarely was she judgemental. There was nothing that she would not do, within her power, for her children and grandchildren. With all that she sacrificed and gave out, all that it took to light up and bring forth her joy and appreciation was a pepsi every day and crabs as often as she could get them.

Rest in eternity, mother, knowing that you were an awesome steward over the lives that God our Father entrusted you with.

Mary Lilly Tucker

Prologue

Finding this book in your possession is no coincidence or mistake so allow yourself the opportunity to reflect and embark upon the freedom journey to finding and becoming the God-created and intended you. I use the word journey because, for some of us, it has been a very overwhelming process. Some people have been afforded the luxury of claiming self-disclosure at a very early place in life. If you find yourself in that category – the road to self-awareness not being challenging – then those of us that have been challenged applaud you. The fact of the matter is that many of us can't claim early victory in that very crucial area of our existence. Numerous trials and errors took us on a course that caused moments of devastation, desperation and confusion. Faced with such circumstances and dilemmas, the question many of us asked ourselves was, "What's the use?" At that moment in time, the easier way out seemed so much more convenient. The forces behind the confusion, at least, fed us those thoughts.

It begins early based upon our need to be cared for and developed because of our inability to be responsible for ourselves. Our need to be protected and validated in the early stages of our development falls into the hands of the surrounding influences. Somewhere down the path we come to realize how flawed and unequipped those that we found ourselves connected to were.

Vulnerable to the forces and powers that were assigned to rob us of our inner ability, which is where our true identity lies, we become subject to control and self-deception. We relinquish ourselves to the subtle demands of that very powerful spirit, by way of our need to be accepted by those around us. The feeling of inferiority empowered those that we deemed successful. Relish the very notion to place people in a position of empowerment because of what we perceived to be outward accomplishments.

Identity theft occurs in the lives of those who are recognized as threats to the agenda of this current earthly power, long before they obtain any material possessions. The purpose of this theft is to lessen – and hopefully cause them to abort – their primary purpose of existence. The entire scheme is about misdirected focus based upon a false identity. Chaos and confusion become the driving forces with the intent to instill failure and a sense of low self-worth. Trapped in an illusion that has appealed to an identity that is so outside of who one is supposed to be, all energy, effort and focus is on who one wants to be.

How convinced one can become of that covert new identity, emerging deeper in the illusion of seeking acceptance for who we now pretend to be. We become secret agents on a mission to avoid our real reality that reveals our true identity, preferring to have knock-off status as opposed to being the unique original.

The "be like" syndrome complexes our decisions which creates consequential dilemmas that ultimately lead to very painful experiences. We settle for the phony accolades and false applause as opposed to positioning ourselves for eternal rewards that are granted to those who embrace self-acceptance and true purpose.

Frankly, I am willing to stake my life on the very fact that no God-created human being set out seeking deception and destruction. The only solution to end this pattern of devastation is to embark on the courageous journey of finding more of our true self and embracing that uniqueness.

Life has a tendency to cause us to engulf ourselves into deep and dark holes. Prayerfully and hopefully, this can be a tool to experience the freedom that we so deserve.

It's spiritual!!!

ARE YOU A COPY OR AN ORIGINAL???

Contents

Contents

It Begins

There is probably not a more fitting place to begin than to emphasize the importance of two of the most controversial topics that humanity is faced with – God and faith. They are, without question in my estimation, the central topics as it pertains to mankind and its existence. Much debate, discussion and defense surround these two vital subjects. Lingering questions, as well as sincere concerns, are the motivating factors for many of these intense and controversial sessions of thought.

The question one must ask is, are these concerns as sincere as they may be based upon man's selfish motivation to prove his intellect? Man has been so infused with this idea to prove how intellectually superior he is, that a genuine desire based upon a true heart for the well-being of humanity has bottomed out. Worldly schools of thought have become the driving forces behind this quest for knowledge. The wisdom of this evil and corrupt system has captivated the minds of the very creation that is most dear and affectionate to the one who began all that has a beginning.

I must inform you that, as the God discussion arises, there will also arise another topic of extreme controversy and that is the subject of religion. There is a strategic strategy that has been conjured up by the very spirit that has a major influence in the condition of the world as we currently know it. The very idea of God and religion being synonymous is a deliberate ploy of Satan to control man's interaction with God. Remember, he is very cunning and crafty in his tactics to intervene in our ability to establish a relationship with the God of the beginning. It has been, and always will be, the Father's desire to develop an intimate relationship with His most prized possession. Every relationship has requirements for the purpose of nurturing it but who better than the parties involved to set the precedence. Relationship was God's mindset long before the formation of man-controlled religion.

The focus is still on the beginning. However, that groundwork was necessary to put it in perspective.

If you are not of the atheist mindset, than suffice it to say that we agree that God is a spirit. It is further valid to say that, as a spirit, He existed long before anything that He decided to create for His purpose and pleasure. Conception began in His mind and material manifestation was a result of those thoughts. With that in mind, it brings me to ponder the schools of thought surrounding the big bang theory and evolution. The requirement for a bang requires at least one substance so the question becomes, where did that substance originate? Where did what we evolve from have its source of existence? There is a popular saying, "I'm just saying." Everything that exists has to have been created, so can a thing be created without a thought? That which "I'm just saying" is out of a sincere desire for awareness, enlightenment and understanding – not to generate another verbal assault for further separation and disharmony (there is enough of that).

With all that being said, the main ingredient required to embrace the God reality is one of those very controversial words known as faith. In looking at this word that has a tendency to be viewed as very complex and confusing, two perspectives come to mind – the dictionary definition and the biblical definition of this word.

Dictionary: Faith - a belief in the value, truth or trustworthiness of someone or something; belief and trust in God, the Scriptures or other religious writings; a system of religious beliefs

I am of a strong persuasion that it was not the intent or purpose of God to impose a religion, but enact a relationship between Himself and that which He created. Religion is so prejudiced by man's opinion of how one must relate and conform in order to get to a loving and inviting God that the task can become so overwhelming, it causes discouragement. Belief and trust in the tangibleness of God is complex enough in and of itself without including man into the equation.

As we take a look at the word faith from a scriptural point of view, it will require the carnal thinking of our human element to be subject to a more spiritual mindset.

Hebrews 11:1 [NIV]

Now faith is being sure of what we hope for and certain of what

we do not see.

Could we be faced with any greater challenge than to believe and trust in what is the source of our creation in spite of the fact that we cannot physically see Him, aside from that which He has produced? How crucial is it to try and wrap one's mind around the notion that my very existence is not centered around my own personal gratification? What a contradiction to the mindset that has been the driving force to a past and present reality. How devastating of an awakening to the falsehood of misinformation received from encountered influences. What a travesty to arrive, after much wasted energy, to the realization that my life is not my own.

The truth of the matter is that it began long before my ability to embrace acceptance of the fact that a source far greater than myself had a purpose and plan in mind when this process was put in place. The responsibility that falls on that which has been created becomes the willingness to line up and perform the service required. The task has been assigned and the necessary tools have been implemented. The trillion dollar question becomes will we be and do what His plan calls for?

Faith requires an active change in a faulty and flawed belief system that was strategically interjected by a spirit bent on creating devastation. The reconditioning of a mindset that resulted in numerous ruinous behaviors to a diligent transformation of the heart. The evidence of our defective belief system, which was the result of faith, was manifested in the wreckage that was present in our lives. We believed wholeheartedly in a system that we bought into out of possible desperation. It became the driving and motivating force on a journey to strip us of our true heritage, character and dignity. Our hope was entrenched in something that meant us nothing but evil, but presented us with all the trappings of accomplishment.

A shift in belief systems has the potential to be very challenging. The faith that was required in the old system was based upon evidence that appealed to fleshly desires and the carnal senses. To now ascribe my existence to an unseen power that one must place all hope in raises a notion for a level of fear. Making the transition from my life being in my hands and control, to now trusting in the Creator that cannot be touched or seen can and will generate some uncomfortability. How shattering to come face to face, based upon all the evidence of the experience of the old reality, that the plan we sold out to was not the original plan at all.

Planned Arrival

Jeremiah 1:5 [NIV]

> *Before I formed you in the womb, I knew you, before you were born I set you apart; I appointed you as a prophet to the nations.*

I strongly remember after being in what could have been a fatal car accident that could have killed my oldest son as well as myself, a very clear and profound voice that I believe to have been the Holy Spirit say these words to me, "People that live on purpose don't have accidents; they have encounters." In spite of the course that my life would take, something in me got a clear revelation that my life and all that I had experienced and would later experience, were part of a plan called purpose.

Long before conception, there was assignment. Chosen before we were given the free will to choose. Purposed for a particular and unique role in His creation. Ordained for success long before being faced with the option to fail. Skillfully and carefully designed to perform a task. Shaped and formed to function as an ambassador of the God of purpose and planning. What was spiritually motivated has been reduced to fleshly and carnal pleasure.

Genesis 1:26-27 [NIV]

> *26) Then God said, Let us make man in our image, in our likeness, and let them rule over the fish of the sea and the birds of the air, over the livestock, over all the earth, and over all the creatures that move along the ground.*
>
> *27) So God created man in his own image, in the image of God he created him; male and female he created them.*

Venture with me for a moment. Remember, this is a walk of faith and I am of strong belief that God honors a sincere heart. Everything began with God first, as a conception in His mind. So let us walk through this from the scriptural beginning of the reformed earth after it was formless and empty.

Genesis 1:2 [NIV]

> *Now the earth was formless and empty, darkness was over the surface of the deep, and the Spirit of God was hovering over the waters.*

Remember the earlier statement concerning a spiritual act that has been turned into fleshly and carnal selfish pleasure? Spiritual intercourse was the motive of the spirit of God as it hovered over the formless and empty earth. Conception through intercourse was enacted by the Creator Himself.

The word conception as defined by Webster: Conception - the union of sperm and egg; a mental thought or plan

The word intercourse as defined by Webster:

Intercourse - mutual exchange between persons or groups; communication; sexual intercourse

There was a very intimate act taking place as the Spirit of God suspended over that which it began to speak to in a very intent and purposeful way. He began to communicate the purpose of His presence. That which He was engaging became His focus. So can it be safe to say that the "Us" was Him and the earth? He communicated the purposed plan of His intimate encounter which resulted in the manifestation of all that He said. At your liberty, read Genesis chapter 1 in its entirety. The arrival of all that He saw was a direct result of a very carefully thought out plan.

Time and effort were put into the planned arrival of man, who was to represent the image and likeness of the Creator. Fashioned and shaped by His most powerful attribute, love. His dominant love trait caused Him to do for man what had not been done for any other act of creation and that was to place him in His hands. The intimacy of touch was instituted as He partnered with earth to bring forth His prized and privileged possession.

Up until the creation of man, all that was manifested was voice-activated.

Genesis 1 [NIV]: God said,

> 3) *Let there be light*
>
> 6) *Let there be an expanse between the waters to separate water from water*
>
> 9) *Let the water under the sky be gathered together to one place, and let dry ground appear*
>
> 11) *Let the land produce vegetation: seed-bearing plants and*

trees on the land that bear fruit with seed in it

14) Let there be lights in the expanse of the sky to separate day from night

20) Let the waters teem with living creatures

24) Let the land produce living creatures according to their kinds

Consider the transition in His communication from these prior verses from let there be to now in verse 26 to let us make.

26) Let us make man in our image, in our likeness, and let them rule [NIV]

The sovereign God, as His Spirit is engaged in this extreme intimate act with that which has been created, has now imparted His image and likeness and now declares to His partner to bring forth the treasured product of their interaction.

The Spirit of God inseminated earth and now the seed of that impregnation is called forth and then fashioned, shaped and given an assignment.

Genesis 2:4-7 [NIV]

4) This is the account of the heavens and the earth when they were created, when the Lord God made the earth and the heavens

5) and no shrub of the field had yet appeared on the earth and no plant of the field had yet sprung up for the Lord God had not sent rain on the earth and there was no man to work the ground,

6) but streams came up from earth and watered the whole surface of the ground

7) the Lord formed the man from the dust of the ground and breathed into his nostrils the breath of life and the man became a living soul.

Man was created and equipped with all the attributes and qualities from a paramount partnership, to produce by way of example. The assignment of being a reflection of the sources of their creation was passed on to them. Fruitfulness and reproduction by way of intimate interaction were the mandate. Instruction for the task was clearly conveyed but somewhere in the captivation of a fitting partner, there was allowed an intrusion by an outside influence.

Early Influences

It is critically essential and of the utmost importance that one has a firm grasp on the origin of their existence. Contrary to the many theories that are in circulation surrounding the arrival and evolution of mankind, to have a belief system other than humanity being created in the image and likeness of Almighty God, the creator of heaven and earth, leaves many in a state of total purposelessness. Perhaps that is the very reason for the decay in moral values and vast deterioration and decline in value and regard as it pertains to human life. Strategic influences have been implemented to combat and circumvent the will and plan of the divine Orchestrater of life.

The battle continues, from that moment up until the very present, to be spiritual in nature. Man's dominion embodies his spirituality and therein the very attack is schemed to rob him of that authority. The spirit of God declared an image and likeness in the decree that was pronounced in Chapter 1, verse 30. "And it was so" became the focus of a very contrived and strategic plan to deceive man of his rightful place by way of identity theft.

Is it any wonder that the very people that are entrusted with the responsibility of shaping and revealing our identity are so consumed with the responsibility of providing us with our everyday needs that instilling and nurturing purpose, unintentionally, are not the primary focus and concern? To no discredit of those assigned to be caretakers and stewards, however the prevailing issues of life are a direct result of the strategic plan to dysfunctionalize the family unit that should be the source of fruitfulness and increase. The family unit was to be the vehicle of reflecting the image and likeness of God in the earth. Productivity and increase was supposed to be a direct result of man thinking and acting out of the mind of God the father. Early in the developmental stage, man was exposed to what was to influence his mindset. It is no coincidence that the family structure of this present age has been so influenced by the dysfunctional decline of the very first family. The inability to pass on healthy and productive values was lost in one single act of disobedience. The present family disarray is a reflection of the identity crisis suffered by Adam and Eve under the crafty influence of a spirit contrary to the will and purpose of Almighty God. Ultimate responsibility falls upon Adam and Eve; however, there lies some accountability with those currently entrusted with stewardship of the family unit. The drive and desperation to provide the basics such as food, shelter and clothing have taken priority over providing identity and purpose.

There is this saying that is popular, "It takes a village to raise a child." But in most cases the village is consumed with the same mindset and, as a result, the message that is passed on creates a lot of confused offspring. For the sake of the argument that those in disagreement might raise to this opinion which is based upon my experience, allow me to say this. The village could have no ill intention but, as a result of the heavy influence of this world and the lack of spiritual insight, the message communicated is infiltrated with total self-centeredness.

The earth was to be filled and increased with the love of God, passed on by man who was to be the reflection of that love. Inundated by an influence that opposed but, on the other hand, knew the power that genuine purpose represented, the awareness of self was imposed and became the detriment to man's inheritance of dominion and subduing the earth. This self-awareness exalted creation instead of the Creator. The revelation of self is not the problem God has; it is when we are disconnected as a result of information that has been communicated by a source of influence that is corrupt and division-driven. When we identify our awareness in connection with who it is that we belong to, then and only then, is our self-awareness not problematic. The understanding and acceptance of identifying who we are positions us to receive what we have access to. Giving, as a result of His love, is at the very essence of all that embracing purpose and authority represents. Man was given all of the nature and character of God from his very conception for the purpose of being the dominant influence in all that was provided for his rulership, based upon his willingness to submit to God's headship. Man was not created for everything but everything was created for him.

Genesis 1:26-29 [NIV]

26) Then God said, Let us make man in our image, in our

> *likeness, and let them rule over the fish of the sea and the birds of the air, over the livestock, over all the earth, and over all the creatures that move along the ground.*
>
> *27) God created man in his own image, in the image of God he created him; male and female he created them.*
>
> *28) God blessed them and said to them, Be fruitful and increase in number; fill the earth and subdue it. Rule over the fish of the sea and the birds of the air and over every living creature that moves on the ground.*
>
> *29) Then God said, I give you every seed-bearing plant on the face of the whole earth and every tree that has fruit with seed in it. They will be yours for food.*

Lodged in embracing self-awareness through our Godly identity is total access to all of God's provisions. Lack has constituted the abandonment of imparting into vulnerable and influential offspring the need to be who they were designed to be.

Many, at a very fragile and impressionable state, have been left for the village to raise and create some type of awareness in us. The village, however, has not been in the spiritual posture to adequately point us in the most healthy direction. The surrounding influences were identical to the dysfunctional homes we came from. Single families, drug dependence, financial instability and abuse in one form or another were the contributing factors to the decay and potential demise of the family structure. Keep in mind that what you are exposed to shapes your thinking at that vulnerable and impressionable stage of young life. How do you look for something different when everything around you resembles the things that are familiar to you?

Environments have the tendency to be the greatest influencers of attitudes and behaviors. It is no coincidence that the most destructive behaviors become the more attractive ones. Deception and distraction are at the root of the plan of the powers contrary to the will of God. The luxury of growing up in seemingly safe neighborhoods was not afforded to a great many of us. (Note that I said seemingly safe environments.) This enemy that we are up against doesn't really discriminate between the hood or the suburbs. To be quite honest, the illusion and trickery might, to a certain extent, be somewhat more covert. Deception is deception no matter what social status one wants to put on it.

Well, if you don t believe me, maybe you will believe the Bible. Wealth and riches were in the house that God established for the first family. Sugar Hill or the hood, the spirit of this world's total focus is to destroy purpose. With that being said, my prior statement concerning some of us not having the luxury of growing up in seemingly safe environments is validated.

Social status, financial stability, degrees or any other form the world deems as success, does not omit or give those in these seemingly fortunate positions a pass. As a matter of fact, the cunning and crafty tactics of the enemy are subtly and strategically being implemented because of a deceptive level of comfort due to an abundance in material gain. Luring the village to a place of complacency as it pertains to who-ness as opposed to what-ness keeps the villagers "wanting to be" rather than becoming who they are supposed to be, covertly placing "wanna be" as priority.

Many villages that are raising children have been

infiltrated by outside forces. Countless numbers have been drawn in and stripped of their God-given identity. The spirit of the infiltrator has robbed and displaced many sons and daughters of their place of authority. The wanna be mentality has overridden the supposed to be identity. Driven by a desire to "be like" as opposed to having a strong stance of acceptance with (I am) who he created me to be. The identity crisis is, however, a direct result of the systematic confused state of many communities (villages).

Mass Confusion

The primary objective of the outside forces that are in direct opposition to the purpose and plan of God is to manufacture a state of confusion for humanity to exist in. Aimlessly driven by selfish motivations to achieve the unfulfilling and ultimately empty trappings offered by the master illusionist. Bombarded with continuous conflict and chaos that are attached to the trappings that the appearance of success seems to offer. The chase and pursuit of what, at a glance, has the potential to be the answer and solution to independent living becomes the source of distraction and despair. Entangled in the illusion of self-gratification, that in the early stages represented a sense of freedom, now has become a major cause of confusion and endless dilemmas. What was presented as a gift has now become the source of much grief. Heartache and pain, as a result of all the energy channeled into the pursuit of what appeared to be, only to find out that outside accomplishments only bring inward contradictions and adversities.

The very villages that so many of us are a product of have been blinded by outside forces that are designed to keep us in a state of mass confusion. It is this confused state that has been designed for the very purpose of robbing the masses of true purpose and identity and then dangling a false sense of success that is the result of pride. The plan is very subtle in its implementation but alluring in its appeal to unregenerated people blinded to their true inheritance, value and authority.

Many of us come from villages that are the results of institutional experimentation. To put it quite frankly, they are projects of study. As much as we would like to avoid and not deal with its true existence, oppression and the need to perpetuate a controlled mindset is still alive and enforced. Think of what many of our housing developments in large inner cities are labeled as, Projects. The idea and focus is to control and contain the growth and development of a group of people that present a threat to the system's agenda if they ever recognize and embrace their true identity and purpose.

We can become so blinded by a religious experience that we miss the bigger picture which depicts this ongoing spiritual battle. Christ has paid the price for our freedom but many have not embraced that freedom and victory because of situations and circumstances they are faced with that keep them trapped by the principalities and powers in place. The scriptures are very clear in its declaration of this battle which those that have not and those that have are faced with. The born again believer is not exempt from the onslaught of spiritual wickedness in high places in spite of being, hopefully, equipped to stand in the face of adversity. Division and control are the project of spiritual opposition.

Project - a collaborative plan that has been carefully designed to achieve a particular aim

"Projects" - a government-subsidized housing development

Does that sound familiar to a group of people that became enslaved many years ago in a place called Egypt? So often we want to downplay this current dilemma that so many are trapped in, which mirrors the situation created in Egypt to promote governmental containment to control the growth and development of a people they feared may one day realize their true potential.

Oppression is actively alive and the awakened must defend those that are yet asleep. Freedom is not the result of taking shackles off of people's hands and feet. It takes place when their hearts and minds are unveiled to the truth of whose they are and who they are. The project of hiding truth that leads to the revealing of identity, which is the primary objective of the oppositions in place, wages on. The awakened must take a stand because they understand the nature of the battle.

Ephesians 6:12 [NIV]

> *For our struggle is not against flesh and blood, but against the rulers, against the authorities, against the powers of this dark world and against the spiritual forces of evil in the heavenly realms.*

Many of the authorities, rulers and powers are under the heavy influence of powerful evil influences that have put a system in place to kill, steal and destroy the drive and ambitions of people created to have authority and dominion.

This is not a conspiracy theory but, in reality, the words of the king of Egypt are still resounding today, "We must deal shrewdly with them." Modern day Egypt is mental oppression and identity awareness.

Exodus 1:8-10 [NIV]

> 8) *Then a new king, to whom Joseph meant nothing, came to power in Egypt.*
>
> 9) *"Look," he said to his people, "the Israelites have become far too numerous for us.*
>
> 10) *Come, we must deal shrewdly with them or they will become even more numerous and, if war breaks out, will join our enemies, fight against us and leave the country."*

The fear of a people awakening to the power that lies in them – becoming aware of their true potential and value – by shrewdly organizing a systematic plan of attack, continues to be carried out. Organized chaos is the strategy of these current powers. Creating the illusion of care and concern by putting in place a welfare system that is ultimately designed for dependence as opposed to self-awareness and constructive development.

Thus were the conditions that the Hebrews were thrust into once a power was put into place that feared their growth and development. Inflicting the nation of Israel with a mentality of rigorous servitude created an attitude of bitterness and resentment. Consider for a moment how confusing the welfare message has the potential to be. Take these handouts that are offered to you; however, there will be imposed hardship placed upon you based upon the possibility that one day your mind might become free to realize your true potential and no longer be in a state of "neediness". Creating a mindset that generates consuming negative thoughts and emotions that lead to behaviors has a more lasting effect than physical bondage can ever have. What slavery to live a life driven by such forces of energy identified as bitterness, anger and resentment.

Exodus 1:14 [NIV]

> *And they made their lives bitter with hard bondage in mortar, in brick, and in all manner of service in the field. All their service in which they made them serve was with rigor.*

Driven by taskmasters who recognize and capitalize off of your potential and gifts, however at the same time, create systems and strategies designed to promote confusion. Building and stabilizing the structures and economies of powers who are terrified at the thought of a people awakening to who they are supposed to be is confusion at its most powerful state.

The death edict has been imposed by the rulers and powers that be. The decree has gone out to the villagers that are to be responsible for the birthing of difference makers, assigned to free the minds of preordained empowered men as well as women. The villagers must now make a determination of whose will is more vital the king's or God's. The requirement for this decision calls for an internal inventory of one's spiritual values. The developing of a leader that has the potential to free a people based upon the challenging choices of another individual's willingness to allow life, confronts the village. If the village is confused about its spiritual condition, many will continue to die.

Exodus 1:15-18 [NIV]

> 15) *The king of Eqypt said to the Hebrew midwives, whose names were Shiphrah and Puah,*
>
> 16) *When you help the Hebrew women in childbirth and serve them on the delivery stool, if it is a boy, kill him; but if it is a girl, let her live.*
>
> 17) *The midwives, however, feared God and did not do what the king of Egypt had told them to do; they let the boys live.*
>
> 18) *The king of Egypt summoned the midwives and asked them, Why have you done this? Why have you let the boys live?*

Who will develop the courage in the face of the king to allow future leaders to live? Is it any wonder, if you take a look closely at most of our government-funded housing developments, that they are filled with males? Yes, there has to be a presence of women, and by no means are they to be discounted. However, in most cases, they have to be single parents in order to occupy these developments. Keep in mind the very important word (PROJECTS). Boys seeking guidance and direction from whatever source of information is available. All too often, they are exposed to influences that have the ability to alter their intended purpose and infuse a wanna be mentality!!! The alluring appeal of the luxuries of existence can so easily replace the desire to live a purpose-driven life.

Dilemmas and Decisions

Many a time in our formative years, the task of making healthy and productive decisions created numerous challenges that usually led to uncomfortable dilemmas. These decisions, based upon influences that were readily available to supply us with inappropriate information when faced with the decision-making process, became a major contributor to the outcome. Countless numbers of individuals, due to the unavailability of positive and insightful direction (through no real fault of their own), have had to make very costly mistakes due to choices. The number of persons that don't have access to godly persons or don't have access to godly spiritual counsel far outweighs those that do. Many are placed in situations as a result of desperation to preserve life. A lot of the decisions that people are confronted with are a direct result of others' fear and self-centeredness. Selfish motives have a direct impact on other people's choices in life. That is not an excuse for bad decision-making, regardless of the reality. The Garden of Eden on behalf of Adam and his wife, Eve, is our prime example. The current dilemma that humanity is faced with is a direct result of the first family's willful disobedience generated from a spirit of wanna be like as opposed to embracing the freedom and authority that came with who they were supposed to be.

Genesis 3:4-5 [NIV]

> 4) *You will not surely die, the serpent said to the woman.*
>
> 5) *For God knows that when you eat of it your eyes will be opened, and you will be like God, knowing good and evil.*

Adam, the free moral agent, was placed among all of God's good; however, he was mandated with the challenge of choice. Confronted with decision-making based upon the appeal of all that was available, would ultimately become his dilemma. To say that it is a no brainer – don't eat and live or eat and die – can be a very easy decision to come to when we are not faced with the circumstances. The true test of a man's character comes to surface in the midst of adversity and appealing influences. Obedience to the choice process for a while seemed very effective for Adam as he operated in his authority amongst God's best. Every formed beast and bird that God created and brought to him, he gave them their identity as he was commanded. The given of God, however, comes with great requirement, struggle and opposition. Consider this scripture for example.

Luke 12:48 [NIV]

> *But he who did not know yet committed things deserving of stripes, shall be beaten with few. For to every one to whom much is given from him much will be required; and to whom much has been committed, they will ask the more.*

We are driven by our lower nature which thrives upon self-centered obsession to receive and is always focused towards wanting and obtaining without ever giving thought to the responsibility, sacrifice, discipline and requirements that are connected to that which is given. Fear, not faith, is the motivating force engineering the desire to gather because of a need to have for security as opposed to having for purpose and stewardship. Totally unaware of the lack of God-dependence to sustain our lives, our ego (enforced by being recognized) along with the sense of empowerment (based upon superficial accomplishments and collection), fuels one's passion for wanting the given.

The given of God comes with much responsibility for healthy decision-making and choices that have the ability to create crucial dilemmas. A loving, kind and secure God the Creator empowered mankind, that is, created him in His image with the freedom to make decisions and choices. Decision-making SHOULD be a direct result of careful consideration and judgement. If you notice, I put great emphasis on the word should. Most often, in times past and the present, decision-making is haphazard or reckless and results from an under-processed mindset. Conclusions are based upon instant gratification without factoring in the consequences connected to a momentary feeling.

The one man, Adam, made a decision that would have dire consequences – not only that would affect him, but all of his lineage. His decision-making was no longer centered around who he was but it was now rooted in the influence of what someone else wanted and his zeal for acceptance. The wanna be spirit was birthed in the garden, the very place that he was supposed to be the one in authority and be the example of God.

Genesis 3:6 [NIV]

> *When the woman saw that the fruit of the tree was good for food and pleasing to the eye, and also desirable for gaining wisdom, she took some and ate it. She also gave some to her husband who was with her, and he ate it.*

Here we have the image of God faced with a decision that no doubt generated a huge dilemma for his emotional state, because of his attachment to the person presenting him with the invitation.

Dilemma - a predicament requiring a choice between equally desirable alternatives

It is so easy to judge a decision that had so many ramifications when one is not faced with the situation. One can come up with all the would've, could've and should'ves that might come to mind, but what would have been the outcome if you were Adam being offered fruit from fine Eve? Remember, he was deeply attracted to that which was conceived out of him. What a predicament to be faced with! The very thing that has captured your heart has now put you in a position to make a decision about something that has appealed to them and they want you to partake in what they are offering you. The emotional attachment to that which is connected to us has much power. The ability to make rational and life-changing decisions clouded by feelings and emotions has the tendency to be overwhelming. This is not a pass for either Adam or ourselves, but an opportunity for awareness, observation and also some sensitivity when faced with the difficulty in decision-making. Judge not!!!

Consequences are, most times, more costly than the momentary rewards of the instant satisfaction that comes along with matters of the heart or the flesh. Once we carry out a decision that we have arrived at, we do not have the luxury of choosing the consequences. How unhealthy for our growth process would it be to make destructive choices and receive productive results? That would be a license to proceed in chaos and confusion. The harsh reality of it all is the fact that we really are not built or equipped to handle the undisciplined decisions that we tend to make. The normal and most frequently used behaviors are blame, finger-pointing and shame-based fear. The garden experience is a prime example of decision-making that led to very severe consequences beyond man's ability to handle so he entered the blame game.

Genesis 3:8-19 [NIV]

> 8) Then the man and his wife heard the sound of the LORD God as he was walking in the garden in the cool of the day, and they hid from the LORD God among the trees of the garden.

> 9) But the LORD God called to the man, Where are you?

> 10) He answered, I heard you in the garden, and I was afraid because I was naked; so I hid.

> 11) And he said, Who told you that you were naked? Have you eaten from the tree that I commanded you not to eat from?

> 12) The man said, The woman you put here with me she gave me some fruit from the tree, and I ate it.

> 13) Then the LORD God said to the woman, What is this you have done? The woman said, The serpent deceived me, and I ate.

> 14) So the LORD God said to the serpent, Because you have

done this, Cursed are you above all livestock and all wild animals! You will crawl on your belly and you will eat dust all the days of your life.

15) And I will put enmity between you and the woman, and between your offspring and hers; he will crush your head, and you will strike his heel.

16) To the woman he said, I will make your pains in childbearing very severe; with painful labor you will give birth to children. Your desire will be for your husband, and he will rule over you.

17) To Adam he said, Because you listened to your wife and ate fruit from the tree about which I commanded you, You must not eat from it, Cursed is the ground because of you; through painful toil you will eat food from it all the days of your life.

18) It will produce thorns and thistles for you, and you will eat the plants of the field.

19) By the sweat of your brow you will eat your food until you return to the ground, since from it you were taken; for dust you are and to dust you will return.

Decisions made out of self-motivated pleasure will always put us in a position to compromise our true position of power. The income does not compare to the devastating outcome. Uncalculated decision-making provoked by a wanna be mentality becomes the origin of fear and vulnerability as a result of a desire to be identified by unauthorized influences. The beauty of our identity was really rooted in nakedness; however, nakedness exposed as a result of guilt and shame created a desperate desire to make a decision to cover the very thing that is supposed to set us apart from all creation. Fear of exposure has driven us to seek cover in the things that God has created as opposed to us covering the things that He has created for us to cover and have dominion over.

What voices are we allowing to influence our decision-making that are driving us into seclusion and isolation? Who is in your ear telling you that it is acceptable to make decisions that will ultimately strip you of your authority? Who is deceiving you to believe that the vision of your true self is shameful, unappealing and without any true value or purpose? Who is feeding you forbidden fruit that will remove you from your assigned place of purpose? Who told you who you were not and you believed them? What decisions are you making based upon misinformation?

It is critical that at some point we develop a discerning ear as it pertains to where our information is being generated from. The messages that we are hearing have a great deal to do with what the motivation and intent of the messenger have been prejudiced by. The message of self-acceptance has been scrambled, confused, manipulated and filled with deception because our environments are inundated with fakes, frauds and phonies.

The wanna be mindset has gripped our existence and, as a result, we have been driven by the obsession to be other than the beautiful and purposed creation that we were destined to become. The transference of an envious and ungrateful spirit has become the driving and prevalent influence in much of our decision-making and the product of many of our dilemmas. In opposition to embracing the beauty of the spoken thought that he was, Lucifer made a decision to adapt and embrace the be like syndrome.

Isaiah 14:12-14 [NIV]

> *12) How you have fallen from heaven, O morning star, son of the dawn! You have been cast down to the earth, you who once laid low the nations!*

> *13) You said in your heart, I will ascend to heaven; I will raise my throne above the stars of God; I will sit enthroned on the mount of assembly on the utmost heights of the sacred mountain.*

> *14) I will ascend above the tops of the clouds; I will make myself like the Most High.*

We don't have to make ourselves to be like God. All that is required is to embrace the thought that we were spoken to be.

WHO IS SPEAKING???

A Spoken Thought

It is imperative that we embrace the true essence of our very existence if we are to be effective in the role that we have been assigned to fulfill. There is a scripture that gives reference to the fact that creation anticipates the revealing of the true offspring of God.

Romans 8:18-19 [NKJV]

> 18) *For I consider that the sufferings of this present time are not worthy to be compared with the glory which shall be revealed in us.*

> 19) *For the earnest expectation of the creation eagerly awaits for the revealing of the sons of God.*

We, the spoken thoughts of the Father of all creation, which were spoken from a heart motivated by true love now find ourselves in a place of utter desperation as a result of defiance and deception. The creative thought process of the Almighty that can only be adopted by faith – because His mind is so beyond our understanding – crafted this material world that we currently inherit.

Even in its current state of chaos and confusion it is the spoken thought of God, the master Craftsman. Contrary to the present evils that seemingly display themselves through all the many suffering deeds, the revealing of the prize of His imagination will ultimately prevail. Careful and strategic planning, not impulsive and reckless unmanageable emotions, were the driving factors in His decision-making. Unmanaged emotions are the reason for our current situation; however, with the Father being the architect of critical thinking it too was factored into the plan. The revealing of His solution to this present dilemma is resoluted in the manifestation of the sons of God which are a product of His spoken thoughts.

Crafted by careful and strategic thinking are those of us that come to believe who we were intended to be. Purposed with a plan of eventual success. Designed to withstand the turmoil of this journey called life. Built to overcome the lure and temptation that comes along with being a living soul. Fearfully and wonderfully made, however, not flawless and without defects and liabilities. The crown of His creation and ultimate weapon in His plan of redemption. Prepared for a future that is so far beyond our ability to comprehend. The Supreme thinker's thoughts are governed by knowledge, insight, understanding and desire.

Jeremiah 29:11-14 [NKJV]

> 11) *For I know the thoughts that I think toward you, says the LORD, thoughts of peace and not of evil, to give you a future and a hope.*
>
> 12) *Then you will call upon Me and go and pray to Me, and I will listen to you.*

13) And you will seek Me and find Me, when you search for Me with all your heart.

14) I will be found by you, says the LORD, and I will bring you back from your captivity; I will gather you from all the nations and from all the places where I have driven you, says the LORD, and I will bring you to the place from which I cause you to be carried away captive.

Critical thinking is paramount in the planning of our eternal place of occupation; therefore, the Father's plan requires us to experience some moments of slavery and captivity and most of it occurs in that powerful place called the mind!!! The thoughts that we think of ourselves and for ourselves, because of our identity crisis, are usually far beneath our privileges as prize possessions. The deceptive influences of the spirit of evil have so infiltrated our thinking that we speak from the position of victim as opposed to victor. We snare our process to prosperity because we embrace the problem and not the solution. The problem being failure to identify the true nature and origin of our identity. We have so settled for listening and agreeing with the second voice conveying to us that we are other than we were created to be. That voice has interjected thoughts of self-worthlessness, less than, be other than, you will never be anybody other than a failure. The list is endless of the fruitless spoken thoughts that are communicated by the deceiver of destinies.

Communication is a vital tool as it pertains to our place in this domain that has been given us to have dominion over. The voice that is adhered to usually results in the actions and behaviors that take place. This question was asked earlier in a different form, "Whose audience have you become?" Any message that is not motivated by the well-being of humanity from a standpoint of love, unity and peace is contrary to the voice of the Original Communicator. The word communication is defined as the exchange of ideas by writing, speech or signals.

The mind is the birthplace of ideas; however, the heart should be the filtering place to examine the motivation and intent of the idea. Growth, maturity, recognition and discipline are the pivotal qualities necessary as it pertains to processing ideas. A mind that has not been developed by these qualities has the potential to be a very dangerous place. It can be a life source or a death trap depending upon the condition of the individual's state of mind and heart. The individual that checks in with the condition and motivation of their heart will have the ability to channel incoming information as well as all other communication from outside sources before acting or speaking upon it. Our outward speech and behavior represent our inward perception the majority of the time. What we think of ourselves is conveyed in the conduct and language that we exhibit. Your communication will expose your thoughts of who you wanna be or who you are supposed to be. Let's not take for granted the power and value of healthy communication.

We need to recognize and embrace the gift that the tool of communication truly is. Communication is expressed in several ways: 1) the body has its own unique language, 2) art has its mood of how it speaks, 3) there is a creative message in music, and 4) we have often heard that money has a way of talking. All of these methods have their value and importance as vehicles of exchanging ideas and information; however, none of the mentioned have the ability to compare to the very systematic order by which the mouth articulated the cosmos into existence. Money matters but money didn't create what matters. Money and everything that exists in this material world are a direct result of thoughts that were spoken by the Master Designer, the Chief Architect, the Ultimate Craftsman and Creator of all that is anything, God the Father.

John 1:1-3 [NKJV]

> 1) *In the beginning was the Word, and the Word was with God, and the Word was God.*
>
> 2) *He was in the beginning with God.*
>
> 3) *All things were made through Him, and without Him nothing was made that was made.*

How can what He determined to exist by way of communicated thought explain His existence?! His beginning predated what He spoke into being; therefore, it lacks the ability to authenticate what caused it to become. All things that be are a direct result of Him speaking them into being. This is a concept that can only be embraced by faith – based upon His existence or origin being beyond human understanding and intellectually unexplainable. There are really no words to accurately communicate the great mystery of His being. What God created lacks insight to affirm His existence; however, it can be an agent to communicate that He is the author of life. The body, art, music and money – all instruments by which a message is relayed – are a product of the mind thinking and the mouth speaking. It was the mouth of the One from the beginning that manifested Himself in the person of Christ that declared the answer to the sin problem, which no other instrument had the ability to answer.

Truth is the instrument that will ultimately lead us to eternal victory. So often, biblical truths are not communicated or interpreted properly and that is by design. However, that being the case, the wrong message is often conveyed as in the case of the interpretation of Ecclesiastes 10:19 which says money answers all things. The preceding verses make mention of the thinking of the foolish and immature leader who looks to outward pleasures to avoid inward realities which point to character weaknesses that result from a lack of wisdom and insight. One who is intoxicated by temporary pleasures to experience self-centered gratification – with the root being misinformed self-awareness. The foolish leader values treasure more than wisdom; therefore, his communication leads to error and corruption.

Ecclesiastes 10:2-3, 12-13, 18-19 [NKJV]

> 2) A wise man's heart is at his right hand, But a fool's heart at his left.
>
> 3) Even when a fool walks along the way, he lacks wisdom, And he shows everyone that he is a fool.
>
> 12) The words of a wise man's mouth are gracious, But the lips of a fool shall swallow him up;
>
> 13) The words of his mouth begin with foolishness, And the end of his talk is raving madness.
>
> 18) Because of laziness the building decays, And through idleness of hands the house leaks.
>
> 19) A feast is made for laughter, And wine makes merry; But money answers everything.

Money, being the powerful communicator that it is, still lacks the ability to answer this current dilemma's consequences. Money has the potential to purchase many gifts; however, it cannot purchase the eternal gift. With that being said, it in no way can be the answer to all things.

Romans 6:23 [NKJV]

> *For the wages of sin is death, but the gift of God is eternal life in Christ Jesus our Lord.*

John 3:16 [NKJV]

> *For God so loved the world that He gave his only begotten Son, that whosoever believes in Him should not perish but have everlasting life.*

Acts 20:28 [NKJV]

> *Therefore take heed to yourselves and to all the church of God which He purchased with His own blood.*

Genesis 5:15 [NKJV]

> *And I will put enmity between your seed and her seed; He shall bruise your head and you shall bruise his heel.*

Christ the only begotten of God, the seed of the woman, the Gift of God by which eternal life is purchased and the revealed thought of the Father is the only "all things" answer to life. It is in this very thought of God that we, as heirs of an eternal Kingdom, can begin to experience the nothing missing, nothing lacking and nothing broken solution to the woes of life that are a direct result of deception.

2 Peter 1:3-4 [NKJV]

> *3) as His divine power has given to us all things that pertain to life and godliness, through the knowledge of Him who called us by glory and virtue,*

4) by which have been given to us exceedingly great and precious promises, that through these you may be partakers of the divine nature, having escaped the corruption that is in the world through lust.

It is not until we come to a heartfelt knowledge of who He is and what He has designed out of love and wisdom for us, that we will break the alluring and lustful trappings of this world gone corrupt. The precious promises of God were carefully and gracefully contrived for His prized possessions. The promises of all things that pertain to life can only be received by those that will embrace the courage to become originals of the divine nature and not continue to be wannabe's that produce fakes, phonies and frauds.

ARE YOU A THOUGHT ORIGINAL OR

A DUPLICATED MIMICKER???

Fakes, Phonies and Frauds

The world that God the Father loves have become masters of deception and phony images posing as something or someone they were not intended to be. The "be like" syndrome has engulfed the minds of that which God loves. The very pride of His creation has digressed from a place of exclusiveness to embracing a mindset far beneath and out of character with the originality that He intended for them. Conforming to a "less than" mentality has taken precedence over the rulership and dominion granted to that which was created in His image. The very likeness of God – as a direct result of deception and trickery – surrendered reflecting God to now taking on a wanna be God position. Lack of acceptance and the infiltration of pride are characteristics that lead to misinformed and counterfeit identities. Lack of self-acceptance and low self-esteem are the breeding ground for ego-inflated complexes. So resounding is the be like message that started in the garden with God's creation that was privileged to experience the nothing missing, nothing lacking and nothing broken lifestyle that comes with acceptance and obedience.

Genesis 1:26-28 [NKJV]

> 26) Then God said, "Let Us make man in Our image, according to Our likeness; let them have dominion over the fish of the sea, over the birds of the air, and over the cattle, over all the earth and over every creeping thing that creeps on the earth."

> 27) So God created man in His own image; in the image of God He created him; male and female He created them.

> 28) Then God blessed them, and God said to them, "Be fruitful and multiply; fill the earth and subdue it; have dominion over the fish of the sea, over the birds of the air, and over every living thing that moves on the earth."

Genesis 2:15-17 [NKJV]

> 15) Then the LORD God took the man and put him in the garden of Eden to tend and keep it.

> 16) And the LORD God commanded the man, saying, "Of every tree of the garden you may freely eat;

> 17) but of the tree of the knowledge of good and evil you shall not eat, for in the day that you eat of it you shall surely die."

Genesis 3:1-5 [NKJV]

> 1) Now the serpent was more cunning than any beast of the field which the LORD God had made. And he said to the woman, "Has God indeed said, 'You shall not eat of every tree of the garden'?"

> 2) And the woman said to the serpent, "We may eat the fruit of the trees of the garden;

> 3) but of the fruit of the tree which is in the midst of the garden, God has said, 'You shall not eat it, nor shall you touch it, lest you die.'"

4) Then the serpent said to the woman, "You will not surely die.

5) For God knows that in the day you eat of it your eyes will be opened, and you will be like God, knowing good and evil."

It is not a mystery that we are in a very intense spiritual battle (not a battle of religious superiority). This battle has everything to do with what authentic identity is and the purpose that is connected to that identity. The plot of the imposing spirit that should be beneath us is to deceive us into desiring to be other than who we are supposed to be which, in turn, causes us to forfeit our rightful authority and inheritance. There is a translation of the scriptures that depicts Satan as a masquerader of an angel of light. He has influenced and enticed many so-called leaders to appear to be so-called men of God but represent a whole different agenda. Disguised to deceive and influence vulnerable individuals away from their place and origin of power.

2 Corinthians 11:13-15 [NIV]

13) For such people are false apostles, deceitful workers, masquerading as apostles of Christ.

14) And no wonder, for Satan himself masquerades as an angel of light.

15) It is not surprising, then, if his servants also masquerade as servants of righteousness. Their end will be what their actions deserve.

2 Corinthians 11:13-15 [NKJV]

13) For such are false apostles, deceitful workers, transforming themselves into apostles of Christ.

14) And no wonder! For Satan himself transforms himself into an angel of light.

15) Therefore it is no great thing if his ministers also transform themselves into ministers of righteousness, whose end will be according to their works.

These two translations use two very thought-provoking words: 1) masquerade, and 2) transform:

Masquerade – to disguise oneself

Transform – to change or alter completely in nature, form or function

To sum both of these words up one can say that something or someone looks like something or someone that they really don't represent. What appears to be is not necessarily what it is. We have become a world of pretenders. It was the late Nat King Cole that wrote a song titled "The Great Pretender". There has even been a slogan adopted which says, "Fake it until you make it." However, there are still those of us that wholeheartedly embrace these words, "There is no future in being a pretender."

It has never been and never will be the will of God for us, His prized creation, to be or appear other than He has designed and desired us to be. He created us individually in such a unique fashion to be a direct expression of His glory. He distinctly fashioned each and every one of us to be an original and not a copy, replica, clone, imitation, duplicate, counterfeit, fake, phony nor a fraud. What a slap in the face or insult of great enormity to the creative ability of the Almighty, All-Knowing, Ever Present, Full of Wisdom architect of all creation to have the audacity to forfeit the you that He called into being in order to become another being that He also created. At this point in my life, with the knowledge and understanding that I have been granted, I wouldn't want to be a culprit of that mindset. I am very sure that any enlightened being, with a hint of fear when it comes to the God of all creation, does not want to find themselves in that position. It is very, very important and imperative when we are in a vulnerable state that we are careful about what becomes the object and focus of our affection.

So we become fixated upon other human beings that have the appearance of what the world or the society that has influenced us deems or identifies as successful. At a glance the outward – based upon our influenced perception – stimulates a desire to wanna be like what is appearing before us. This image, because of our fractured spiritual condition, sparks a desire and motivation to seek after it based upon very limited knowledge and understanding. Scripture reveals to us that it is not zeal and determination in going after a desired thing that is the problem; however, it is the focus and seeking without the proper knowledge and understanding that creates enlightenment which constitutes the problem. So often, our desires and motivations are a result of fleshly and soulish ambitions. We tend to gravitate to the earthly more so than the heavenly. It is not until we somewhat reach a place of spiritual maturity and are able to properly identify with sent role models, examples and mentors that we then can discern the help from the unhealthy. We learn to embrace and have gratitude for the help without being overly consumed with a desire to forsake our own true identity to take on an identity that is far from who God the Father had in mind for us.

Webster's defines the word zeal as great interest or eagerness.

Strong's Exhaustive Concordance defines it as a

feeling for or against; affect, covet and a desire.

Affection and desire uninspired by the Holy Spirit will invoke a hunger and thirst to pursue after the wrong image and likeness which, in turn, alters one's course of life. Anything that captivates the focus of our attention becomes empowered to influence thinking and behavior. The thought process is so very paramount in the lifestyle of the believer. To empower the wrong influences makes one subject to making unhealthy life decisions. Where we place our affections can be very costly if they are not based upon the proper knowledge and understanding, even as it pertains to our Heavenly Father.

Romans 10:2 [NKJV]

> For I bear them witness that they have a zeal for God, but not according to knowledge.

Having an inadequate perception of God has the potential to cause one's focus to be blinded from true purpose and reality. Hunger and thirst, without the proper discipline of wisdom and understanding, have the ability to open up a world full of confusion. Confusion is the polar opposite and in direct opposition to order, which is the nature and character of God. Confusion tends to create its own misconception of a false reality. Vulnerability, without the necessary nurturing and direction, becomes an open invitation for deception and confusion's way in. The pathway to the human heart is often based upon want, need and desire – especially in the longing for validation state. That individual becomes an unsuspecting volunteer for unexpected pain and hardship. The need to be validated, established upon misinformation and a desire to be a part of, becomes the breeding ground for distraction and disappointment.

This type of mentality has the tendency to put and build undeserving people and things in a place of empowerment that they don't rightly deserve. It is the very cunning and crafty method carefully thought out by the master of deception himself to systematically lead astray a nation of kings and queens. Surrendering to a lower standard mentality as opposed to striving to achieve greatness and uniqueness.

Ponder over these three words if you will for a moment:

Fake - not genuine; counterfeit; forgery; sham

Phony - fraudulent; imposter; bogus

Fraud - wrongful deception intended to result in personal gain; claiming to be other than it is

In the movie, Transformers, they had a name for the thing that looked like one thing but really was intended for the sole purpose to deceive. It was labeled a decepticon.

The spirit that has been allowed to rule and dominate this world has raised up a nation of decepticons breeding at a very rapid pace. The minds of many are so engulfed with the appearance of success and accomplishments and gain, it has blinded them to the ultimate end result. Profit and gain of precious metal, wood, cloth, flesh, stone, etc. become the idols of worship.

Listen to what Jesus said regarding worldly profit orchestrated by ungodly purpose and motive.

Mark 8:36 [NKJV]

> *For what will it profit a man if he gain the whole world and loses his own soul?*

It is the arrogance and god complex of man in his deceived state of mind that has led to a self-dependent and idol-worshipping condition. The ego trip is a long journey to an eternal place called suffering.

WHAT IMAGE HAVE YOU RAISED UP???

Ego's Idols

The mind, in its original state, was a gift from the Giver with the intent of it being a place of constructive, productive and creative expressions of the creation created in the image of the Creator. It was designed to represent the creative thoughts of a selfless, loving and caring nature. Intellectual thoughts purposed to be incorporated into this awesome gift called life for the growth and development of humanity's authority in the earth. The freedom to think, speak and see for the purpose of furthering and developing a healthy and productive environment in which man, the prize creation of the Creator, would thrive and subdue that which was fashioned to be under their authority. The mind was formed to think and manifest thoughts which are conceived, therein taking dominion over it and not being subject to the thing that was thought. (A statement to remember – all that is seen is a direct result of a concept that was birthed by a thought – unless you embrace the theory that things or existence are a result of elements forming them with no real purpose [the theory of evolution].) Growth and development should be the motivating factor for creative thinking. The desire to move and usher humanity into a unified purpose.

If the mind, in its vast capacity to generate a thought, produces a thought that is not governed by wisdom, obedience and understanding; it has the potential to become a detriment to our well-being and position with the Almighty. What a powerful tool that has been granted! The ability to take a small seed of thought and expand it into tremendous life-producing existence. It is an instrument that has the ability to produce life-giving resources as well as an agent of death. The thoughts that are filtered through this divine gift must be divinely disciplined. The ability to mature, develop and reach unimaginable heights resides in this place of power and authority. Freedom to shape and produce that which is pleasing to the Creator is contained in that which He created. This mind can generate one thought that has the potential to incite a collaboration of awesome and magnificent works all to the glory of God or to His dismay as well.

This vehicle has the potential to be the ultimate weapon for experiencing freedom but also, in turn, has the ability to become a thinking trap. Thoughts entertained with impure and self-centered, godless motives are likely to be the breeding ground for self-serving monuments. It all begins with a thought. And if that thought is not governed by the Spirit of God, it can become the idol of our affection. Remaining connected to the All is paramount to our existence because, in our quest to be validated, a productive thought manifested could harvest a superiority complex that develops an over-inflated ego.

The casting down of Lucifer only took one "I will" thought that was a direct result of ego-induced thinking motivated by a contrary will of the heart to build in a place that was not meant for him to construct in. It was the seed of wanna be planted in the mind of the most beautiful and gifted creation at that time that caused his demise. If not properly grounded in a posture of humility, accomplishments have the potential to lead to demise. One's over self-indulgence, based upon recognized giftedness and achievements, could be the breeding ground for seeds of arrogant self-righteousness as well as self-motivated over-importance. How can the thing that is thought of become greater and of more importance than that by which it was created?

Romans 12:3 [NKJV]

> *For I say through the grace given to me, to everyone that is among you, not to think of himself more highly than he ought to think, but to think soberly, as God has dealt to one a measure of faith.*

Romans 1:18-32 [NKJV]

> *18) For the wrath of God is revealed from heaven against all ungodliness and unrighteousness of men, who suppress the truth in unrighteousness,*
>
> *19) because what may be known of God is manifest in them, for God has shown it to them.*
>
> *20) For since the creation of the world His invisible attributes are clearly seen, being understood by the things that are made, even His eternal power and Godhead, so that they are without excuse,*
>
> *21) because, although they knew God, they did not glorify Him as God, nor were thankful, but became futile in their thoughts,*

and their foolish hearts were darkened.

22) *Professing to be wise, they became fools,*

23) *and changed the glory of the incorruptible God into an image made like corruptible man and birds and four-footed animals and creeping things.*

24) *Therefore God also gave them up to uncleanness, in the lusts of their hearts, to dishonor their bodies among themselves,*

25) *who exchanged the truth of God for the lie, and worshipped and served the creature rather than the Creator, who is blessed forever. Amen.*

26) *For this reason God gave them up to vile passions. For even their women exchanged the natural use for what is against nature.*

27) *Likewise also the men, leaving the natural use of the woman, burned in their lust for one another, men with men committing what is shameful, and receiving in themselves the penalty of their error which was due.*

28) *And even as they did not like to retain God in their knowledge, God gave them over to a debased mind, to do those things which are not fitting;*

29) *being filled with all unrighteousness, sexual immorality, wickedness, covetousness, maliciousness; full of envy, murder, strife, deceit, evil-mindedness; they are whisperers,*

30) *backbiters, haters of God, violent, proud, boasters, inventors of evil things, disobedient to parents,*

31) *undiscerning, untrustworthy, unloving, unforgiving, unmerciful;*

32) *who, knowing the righteous judgment of God, that those who practice such things are deserving of death, not only do the same but also approve of those who practice them.*

It is not the faith to embrace who we are and then operate in the realm of our limitations that presents us with the wrath of our Creator; however, it is that narcissistic attitude and mentality of over self-importance and self-reliance that becomes our idols of worship. A developed sense of superiority and control which lacks humility and obedience takes precedence over the dominion that we were granted and we now want to erect something greater. These erected things become the object of our affections and the drive behind our motivation. If our hearts are not grounded in humble self-awareness and a true sense of identity, worth and value that is rooted in God-consciousness, we will find ourselves seeking validation in outside constructions. What we develop on the inside has far more sustainability for our personal growth and maturity as opposed to outside measurements of faith. When we grow and present ourselves as worthy vessels to the God of our existence, that is far more honorable than any idol we could ever erect.

Narcissism is defined as an inflated sense of self-importance.

The idea of negotiating or debating with God over that which our narcissistic, self-centered, ego-inflated, self-righteous minds have conceived that now obstructs our vision and insight is absolutely out of the question. There is not a person, place or thing that deserves the place of highest honor in our heart other than the true and living God.

Deuteronomy 5:7-9 [NKJV]

7) You shall have no other gods before Me.

8) You shall not make for yourself a carved image any likeness of anything that is in heaven above, or that is in the earth beneath, or that is in the water under the earth;

9) you shall not bow down to them nor serve them. For I, the LORD your God, am a jealous God, visiting the iniquity of the fathers upon the children to the third and fourth generations of those who hate Me,

The Almighty is very emphatic concerning this commandment or principle (whatever you choose to label it). There is nothing that your mind can conceive or that your hands can construct that should obstruct your awareness, vision or affection to recognize Him as the Most High. Whatever materials that are available to mankind be it wood, stone, metal, water, etc. have all been furnished by His divine wisdom. None of these things or inanimate objects have the ability to think; however, they possess the overwhelming powerful ability to influence mankind's thinking.

Flesh, in that regard, because of its proven ability to be vulnerable and influenced must and has to be inclusive when it pertains to being placed in a position of worship. The inflated ego of flesh that is not spiritually grounded is subject to powerful influential outside forces that are contrary to the well-being of mankind. The egocentric mindset is driven by selfishly-motivated ambitions as opposed to a common good for mankind's advancement. Flesh that is so consumed with its own loftiness and grandiose agenda desires to be placed in a seat of honor above others as well as the Almighty.

Ego - the self-thinking, feeling and acting distinct from the external world; the conscious aspect that most directly controls behavior; self-obsession

Egocentric thinking, observing, and regarding oneself as the center of all experiences; self-centered

There is a very fitting acronym for this word:

Edging
God
Out

It is an egregious offense to the True & Living God as well as a disservice and a detriment to ourselves and whoever and whatever we place in the God box. There is a place that is solely reserved for the dwelling of the Almighty and removing Him is a very unhealthy, hazardous and risky option. The odds of anything or anyone existing in that place more than likely should not be considered; but unfortunately, there are many that will try and defy the odds. It would be in our best interest to be very conscious of any and every thing that would become the focus of our passion and, in turn, obstruct our vision and attention away from Him that is deserving of our affection.

Pride is one of the primary hindrances to obedience; therefore, that idol and anyone that represents that idol must be removed from its place of influence. There was once a king that did what was right in the sight of God until pride was lifted up in his heart and his decision-making became self-serving which led to transgression against God and ultimately destruction. Ego created the idol of pride based upon the recognition of accomplishments and attainments.

2 Chronicles 26:3-5, 16 [NKJV]

> *3) Uzziah was sixteen years old when he became king, and he reigned fifty-two years in Jerusalem. His mother's name was*

Jecholiah of Jerusalem.

4) And he did what was right in the sight of the LORD, according to all that his father Amaziah had done.

5) He sought God in the days of Zechariah, who had understanding in the visions of God; and as long as he sought the LORD, God made him prosper.

16) But when he was strong his heart was lifted up, to his destruction, for he transgressed against the LORD his God by entering the temple of the LORD to burn incense on the altar of incense.

Achievements and accomplishments as well as attaining things are what God wants for us; however, the problem resides with where we place those things and the attitudes and behaviors that are erected. The Almighty's issue with mankind is not with us having and doing but it is with what things have us doing as a result of having them. There are two questions that we must honestly confront ourselves with: 1) Do we have things or do things have us? and 2) What influence has been raised up in your life that is obstructing you from seeing the supposed to be YOU?

Revelation of ME

Of all the crises that humanity has been faced with, the identity crisis has been one of the most damaging as it pertains to us taking our rightful place in the earth. From the moment man, the very affection of the eyes of God, was placed in this earth to rule and have dominion, a plan was conceived to trick and deviate him from the understanding of who he really is and whose he is. Ignorance to the truth of identity leads to unfulfilled destiny and purpose that results in perishing without receiving the promises of the Almighty.

Hosea 4:16 [NKJV]

My people are destroyed for the lack of knowledge,

The lack of the proper knowledge concerning our rightful identity is one of the most powerful tools the rulers of darkness use to deceive and destroy humanity. The enemy places the blinders of truth over our eyes in the form of many outside influences as well as escorting people into our lives that have no real purpose other than to keep us ignorant of the truth of our identity.

Identity assassins have been assigned to us upon our very entrance into this world. Aware of the impact that we possess to be positive influencers of change; agents have been placed on post to hinder our progress by way of fake and deceptive information and the withholding of knowledge. A great many of these vessels of dishonor are not even aware of the harmful damage they are causing due to their ignorance of their own identity. The identity crisis has the potential to have the domino effect because one ignorant person transfers ignorance to another person and the process continues. There is a passage of scripture that states we entertain angels unaware. How about the same is true when it comes to demons?

Hebrews 13:2 [NKJV]

> Do not forget to entertain strangers, for by so doing some have unwittingly entertained angels.

2 Corinthians 11:13-14 [NIV]

> 13) For such people are false apostles, deceitful workers, masquerading as apostles of Christ.
>
> 14) And no wonder, for Satan himself masquerades as an angel of light.

Even in times of vulnerability and uncertainty in our lives, we will be positioned to sow life-giving seeds into the lives of people that we have no clue of who they are. However, our paths have crossed by divine appointment because of something in us that has to be passed on. Likewise, in that very vulnerable and uncertain state, imposters and masters of deceptions and disguises actively are seeking us out to sow seeds of destruction and discouragement into our lives. Vulnerability and uncertainty are a direct result, in most cases, of a lack of knowledge and information. The word ignorance has a very strong tendency to be offensive to us even though it means nothing more than a lack of knowledge and information. The truth of the matter is that all humanity regardless of your academic achievements, extensive education or whatever worldly information we have obtained experiences the reality of ignorance. Let us not allow our egos to charge us with refuting this fact. There is only one that possesses all knowledge, information, wisdom and understanding and that is the Almighty Eternal God Himself.

The only remedy that will combat and be victorious over this conspiring, deceptive plan to rob mankind of his rightful and entitled place is a spiritual awakening. This battle is impossible to overcome from a worldly-educated perspective. The unshakable truth is that the wisdom and knowledge of this world is in direct opposition to the spiritual matters of the kingdom of God. Yes, there are the temporary rewards that come along with worldly achievements but they have no eternal benefits for the soul of man. The things of this world possess the potential to covet our affection and drive us to the brink of possible destruction if we don't develop the balance that is necessary to handle and place these things in their proper place.

Mark 8:36 [NKJV]

> *For what will it profit a man if he gains the whole world, and lose his own soul?*

We live in an era where individuals that have been deemed successful – as a result of those that stand to benefit the most – have polarized these personalities and paraded them and labeled them as role models. There is no issue in celebrating their achievements and whatever accompanies their skill level; however, many of us (and more than likely many of them) would agree that role model status should be merited upon more than a skill level. Gifts and talents coupled with public approval and accolades are the sure ingredients for the god complex.

We must not allow the skilled and talented individual that could possibly be suffering from the very same dilemma that many are suffering from – that being the identity crisis – to become the idol of our attention and affection. That very talent could be the disguise for their lack of internal understanding and revelation of the true person that they really are. Countless gifted people are blinded to the reality of the Giver of the Gift. I reigns over He because their inner awareness has been eroded because of fame and acclaim. The point of the matter is that what they have been skilled, gifted and enabled to do is not who they are. Titles and labels should not and were not designed to represent who we are as spirit beings having a human experience. What happens when the physician can no longer practice, the lawyer can no longer represent, the singer can no longer sing, the athlete can no longer perform, the business man can no longer run the business, the politician can no longer politic or when the preacher can no longer preach? Does life stop because they can no longer participate in the gift and now they just exist or maybe they were just existing and unaware of their self-worth the entire time. Just maybe the time has arrived that we remove these polarized personalities that have been positioned in a place of idolization. Let's not wait for the manifestation of their weakness to temptation, the eventual lure of compromising appetites and their fallibility to making destructive choices, wherein we fall apart because of their offenses and now become judgmental. The truth of the matter is that once their faults and failures are exposed and they are no longer profitable, raised up images to the powers that be, their removal is inevitable. We should find it wise – before these events that have the potential to shake our emotional world based upon our unfair and unrealistic expectations – to remove them before this occurs.

Our keys to freedom were not intended and should not be placed in the hands of another being that is experiencing this human experience. There is a huge price that is required to be paid for our personal freedom. The question becomes, are we willing to develop the courage to pay the price? There is really no great price to pay as it pertains to us focusing on other individuals' journeys through life. Especially those people we see that are not measuring up to our standards, which gives us a sense of feeling that we possibly have arrived. There is a level of shallowness connected to the mindset and school of thought that thinks they should be the measuring tool for someone else's process. The courageous person will suffer and pay the price of placing the focus inward as opposed to being stuck outwardly gazing. Humanity's real value is really not always visible to the eyes. Spiritual discernment and insight allow us to view from a vastly different perspective.

It is of paramount importance that we remove the many personalities and characters that we have implemented to represent and cover up who we really are. Granted, many obstacles have caused this cover up and many of us have cried victim for long enough.

Victimization, at some point, becomes a cop-out and the real truth is that we have taken on the role of volunteer.

Victim - a person harmed, injured, or killed as a result of a crime, accident or other event or action; a person who is tricked or duped or preyed upon

Volunteer - one who offers himself for a service of his own free will; to take part freely

At what point are we willing to stop playing the victim card as well as assuming the role of volunteer? The latter role really and truly has no benefits or rewards because we give ourselves freely with unfair expectations. How sad a place to find oneself in and lack the ambition and courage to make another choice.

The revelation of the real authentic you will unlock doors and remove the shackles and blinders that have held us captive for too long. For many of us, the bondage has been in the form of making lifestyle choices that required us to create images and characters to fit into these lifestyles. These roles become so embedded in our lives because of the length of time that we participated in these destructive behaviors. We had to develop characteristics and survival tools in order that we would not be consumed by the environments and behaviors that come with these lifestyles. We found the acceptance that we so long for in spite of having to hide the fear that accompanied our sense of choosing to be a part of something that would ultimately result in tremendous pain. With the camouflaging of our fear, a false sense of courage and self-inflated ego emerged.

Change requires courage because there exists an extreme level of uncomfortability when it pertains to the unknown and unfamiliar. In spite of all the obvious signs that point towards unproductivity and unfulfillment due to the fact that there will never be success in portraying someone other than the person that you are supposed to be, courage and desire are a must. The courage to tell yourself that I have been perpetrating a fraud for far too long and now the time has finally come that I embrace the authentic me that God has created me to be. Layers and layers of painful truths based upon years and years of unconfronted lies must be exposed and dealt with.

The unveiling and unmasking that will now expose and reveal the true gift that we were designed to be is a process that requires much patience and determination. Patience, because there are many layers of misinformation that created the phony images that must be dealt with. Survival principles that covered our fears and weaknesses must be discarded in a strategic manner because of the level of sensitivity that they generate. Those walls that we created to guard our feelings and emotions must be carefully broken down. Patience, because the letting go of the very thoughts and behaviors that made us acceptable must now be replaced by a whole new mindset. Determination, because if change was easy, everyone would be willing to do it. The forces of control that once operated in our lives must be met with determination because they will no longer possess the influence that they once had. A determined focus must confront old acquaintances and personalities that are sure to resurface with the goal in mind to hinder our supposed to be journey.

Let us now with confidence, courage and humility embrace our supposed to be inheritance; because in doing so, we become images of change for victims that are seeking freedom from the identity crisis of the wanna be battle.

Psalm 4:3 [NKJV]

But know that the Lord has set apart for Himself him who is godly, the Lord will hear when I call unto him.

Jeremiah 1:5 [NKJV]

Before I formed you in the womb, I knew you; Before you were born, I sanctified you; I ordained you to be a prophet to the nations

Romans 8:19-21 [NKJV]

19) For the earnest expectation of the creation eagerly waits for the revealing of the sons of God.

20) For the creation was subjected to futility, not willingly, but because of Him who subjected it in hope;

21) because the creation itself also will be delivered from the bondage of corruption into the glorious liberty of the children of God.

For those of us that have prevailed through the many hardships of life's experiences due to the grace of Almighty God, the time for revealing has arrived. Love and grace, based upon ordination long before conception and birth, overshadowed us through our many painful experiences that resulted from our inability to make healthy decisions for our lives. The assignments that awaited us were preceded by experiences that would shape our ability to embrace many casualties of this battle to freedom. Many of us did not receive the compassion, empathy, sensitivity, patience, guidance or support we may have thought we needed. It, however, now becomes the responsibility of those of us that have overcome great odds that caused us many emotionally painful encounters to be in position to be reflections of hope for the struggling.

There are those of us that must come face to face with the heart-wrenching reality that the prosperity that so often was within our grasp, however so often eluded us in a world full of chaos, confusion and contradiction was not at all intended for us to obtain. On the contrary, the true value of those traumatic encounters is the eye-opening awareness and knowledge that we have the potential to be endowed with. These are the rewards that prosper us in our purposed awakening to the supposed to be seeds of encouragement and enlightenment that we're assigned to be.

We must not disregard the journey that has brought us to our present now as if it were a puzzle of unsolved mysteries, but recognize it as the needed source to motivate a healthy awareness. We must not be shameful of the scars that these engagements inflicted us with, but in stark contrast we must possess the courage to expose these wounds to the doubters of change that we will confront. The time has arrived for the hope agents to allow themselves to be vulnerable enough to be uncovered and touchable. Humility of heart is the primary characteristic as opposed to an attitude of infallible, ego-inflated arrogance.

The emphasis must no longer be placed upon broken, susceptible and eventual failures due to their own appetites and desires when faced with temptation. All flesh, regardless of accomplishment, title or whatever has caused them to be placed in a position of elevation. There is no exception!!! The ultimate end of this type of unrealistic expectation results in emotional devastation and judgement. That is not to say that the accomplishments of man don't deserve a level of honor and respect, but even that has to be within some confines.

Muhammad Ali once adopted the slogan that he was the greatest. He declared this over a period of time until at some point, being the spiritual man that he was, the revelation that he was placing himself in a position with God awakened him and he no longer declared that statement. There are so many, in different arenas, being tagged with the label of the GOAT which means the greatest of all time. Many will contend that it just means the greatest as it pertains to their craft or field of expertise, but the truth of the matter is it generates a mindset of comparison. With that type of mindset, there comes the mentality of I wanna be greater than someone else.

Greatness resides within each and every one of us. However, it cannot be obtained by outward focus and ambitions. It is not a superficial attainment. The uncovering and becoming acquainted with that greatness is an inside job and the opposition and adversary of any meaning that needs to be opposed is that wanna be that has not been evicted from its place of habitation – which is our most prized treasure – the heart. How willing are we to confront and remove that which has the ability to keep us from becoming the greatest me of all time.

This greatest you or me of all time is not achieved or decided by the opinions or ballots of outsiders; however, it is an inside engagement. A vast majority of us, by virtue of painstaking and heart-wrenching results of choices that were made in pursuit of prosperity and success that resulted in much chaos, confusion and contradiction have made a decision to check in before we check out. Faced with the evidence of potential pain and destruction to come and becoming aware of the gift granted by a loving God to make healthier enlightened decisions, we have chosen a more conscious path. This new insight and awareness gives us the benefit and rewards of making better, enlightened choices for our lives that result in less pain and remorse. We become more and more conscious of the destruction and havoc imposed by our self-centered, ego-inflated lower nature. We begin to desire far greater and productive results in the environments that we have been chosen to influence.

The combination of our gifts, experiences and pain become the ingredients that give us the potential to impact and influence whoever and whatever we have been assigned to do. We must awaken to the possibilities that lie ahead of us and not remain paralyzed by the pain that we have encountered along the journey. Our experiences were designed to develop some characteristics that would be preparation for greatness. We are not the devastation of our mistakes; however, we are the proof that overcoming the odds of difficult circumstances and situations is possible. I become the greatest me of all time by confronting my challenges and not allowing my challenges to change me to be anything or anyone other than the me that pleases the Almighty God who designed and created me for His purpose.

There is no better time than NOW to accept and embrace YOU. Let go of what you did or didn't do yesterday and the negative thoughts that you possibly hold of yourself. Grab hold of this present moment that is full of so many possibilities as a result of God's gift called today. Speak life to yourself and all that is attached to you. Be open to positive communication and whatever opportunities come about that will develop character and integrity.

Two thoughts that are very simple, I have heard in my travels:

1. Why not be you, everyone else is already taken?
2. Nobody can beat you at being you.

The greatest you of all time becomes a direct result of accepting and embracing the masterpiece that the Master has created. The good and bad, the assets and liabilities, the brokenness and the restored, the defeats and victories are all necessary ingredients in the process – channeling our energy and actions towards fulfilling our purpose for accepting this space in time. The voice of the overcomer is waiting to be heard!!! The life-speaking voice that will address the pains, ills, afflictions and bondages that society has placed upon so many people awaits our awakening to consciousness.

Entitlement + Enlightenment = Empowerment

www.ingramcontent.com/pod-product-compliance
Lightning Source LLC
LaVergne TN
LVHW051156080426
835508LV00021B/2657